The Short-sighted Hippopotamus

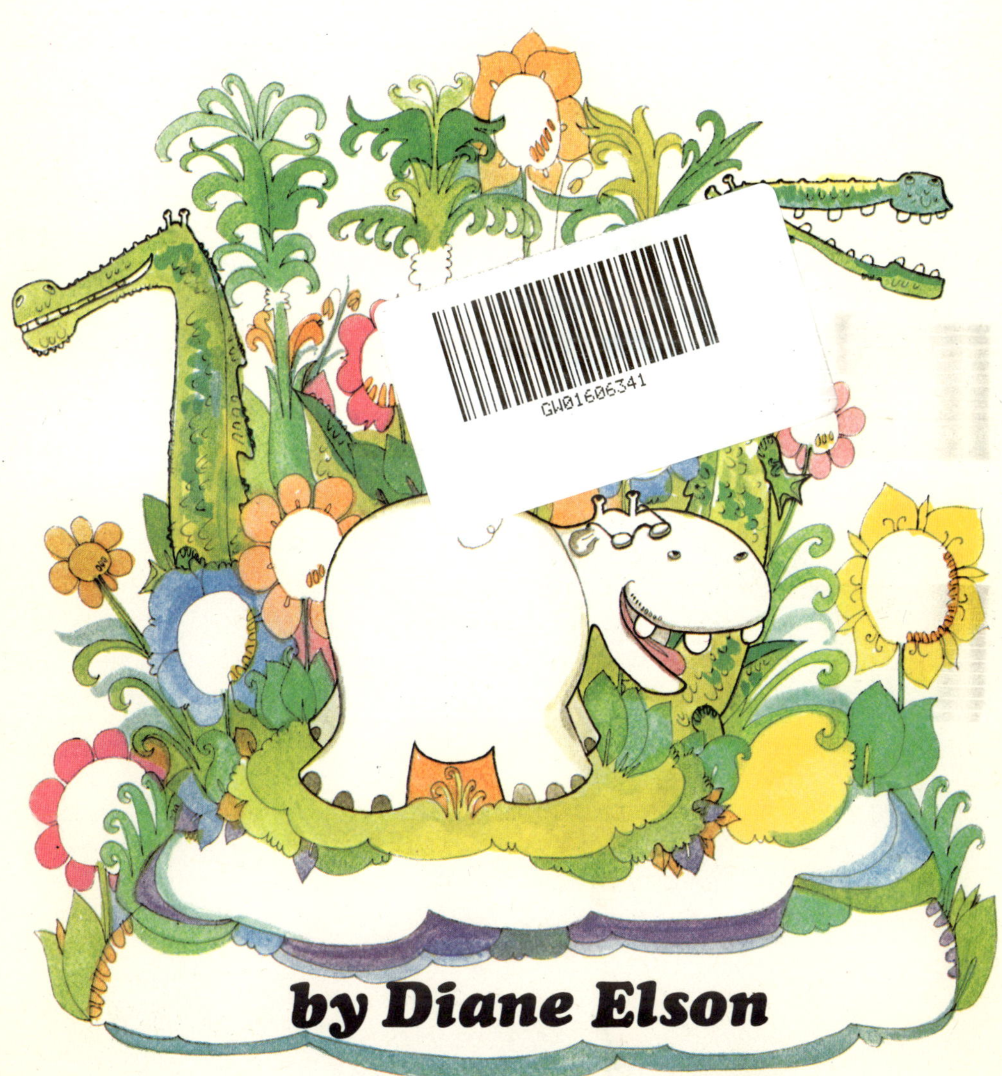

by Diane Elson

Beaver Books

Once upon a time in the jungle there lived a family of Hippopotamuses.

There were three of them – Mother Hippo whose name was Ermintrude, and Father Hippo whose name was William, and Baby Hippo, whose name was Horace. He was three years old and he had three teeth, one for each of his birthdays. He had little brown eyes and a big pink tongue just like his mother and father.

They all lived very happily in the jungle pool,

eating lots of plants and taking mud baths.

Horace had two friends, Charlie and Cedric the two Baby Crocodiles. They were two years old and had twenty teeth.

They liked to play blind hippo's buff

and follow-the-crocodile.

But their favourite
game of all was
leap-frog.

They played leap-frog
every afternoon.

And every afternoon Horace fell over the Crocodiles' tails on to his nose.

And if he didn't fall over their tails he jumped on them instead.

Charlie and Cedric tried again and again to play leap-frog, but each time Horace fell over their tails or his own feet.

In the end the two Crocodiles decided not to play with Horace any more, and went to play with Thomas the Turtle instead.

Poor Horace felt very lonely and unhappy. He just wandered about the pool, talking to himself and singing a sad little song.

Ermintrude heard him and was very sorry for him. She and William decided to ask Henry the Lion for his help.

So that afternoon they went to see Henry, to ask his advice about Horace.

Henry was very thoughtful when they told him the trouble. Then he disappeared into his house.

Henry rummaged in his belongings until he found what he was looking

for. Then he came back to William and Ermintrude.

He was smiling and wearing two funny round things, joined together with wire. They had never seen anything like them before.

Ermintrude tried them on, and they all laughed. 'You look so funny in spectacles, Ermintrude,' said Henry.

Ermintrude and William looked puzzled. 'What are spectacles?' they said.

'You're wearing them,' said Henry. 'They're for Horace because he's so short-sighted. That's why he fell over Charlie and Cedric and trod on Thomas the Turtle.'

‘Short-sighted,’ said William. ‘Poor Horace, no wonder he kept falling over everything.’

And so the two Hippopotamuses
thanked Henry the Lion.
And taking the spectacles
with them, they went home.

Horace put the spectacles on and he could see clearly for the first time in his life. His mother, his father, Charlie and Cedric the Baby Crocodiles, and Thomas the Turtle.

He was so happy he danced round and round the jungle pool, singing and laughing.

All his friends joined in because they were delighted that Horace the Baby Hippopotamus was happy again.

Membership Application Form

Please write clearly (Block letters) using a ballpoint pen and send to **Junglies Club, Wildlife, Wallington, Surrey SM6 0DN.**

Up to 12years of age,
UK & Eire, £1.25 per year.
Overseas, £1.75 per year.

I enclose a postal order/cheque for £.................................
and wish to be registered as a member of the Junglies Club.

Name...

Age ....

Address ....

....

....

Town ....

County..

....

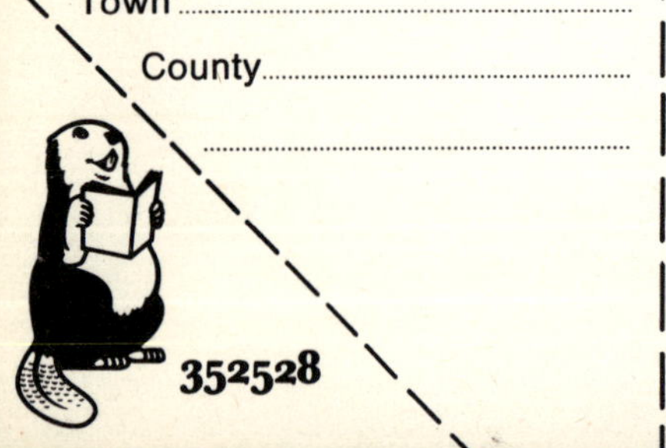

W·Y·S

Administered by the Wildlife Youth Service of the World Wildlife Fund

Henry the Lion says to all boys and girls

Join the Junglies Club and help to save world wildlife

As a member of the Junglies Club you will receive a super badge and membership card together with your own quarterly magazine 'The Junglies Jabber' which will be packed with interesting articles about wildlife and wild places, together with Junglies stories and exciting competitions which will help you to understand wildlife in danger.

As a member of the Junglies Club, you will be helping animals in two ways. Firstly, by helping to support the work of saving wild animals and wild places and secondly, by beginning to learn lots of things about wild animals and why they are in danger of dying out.